Attainment's

# EXPLORE
# Social Skills

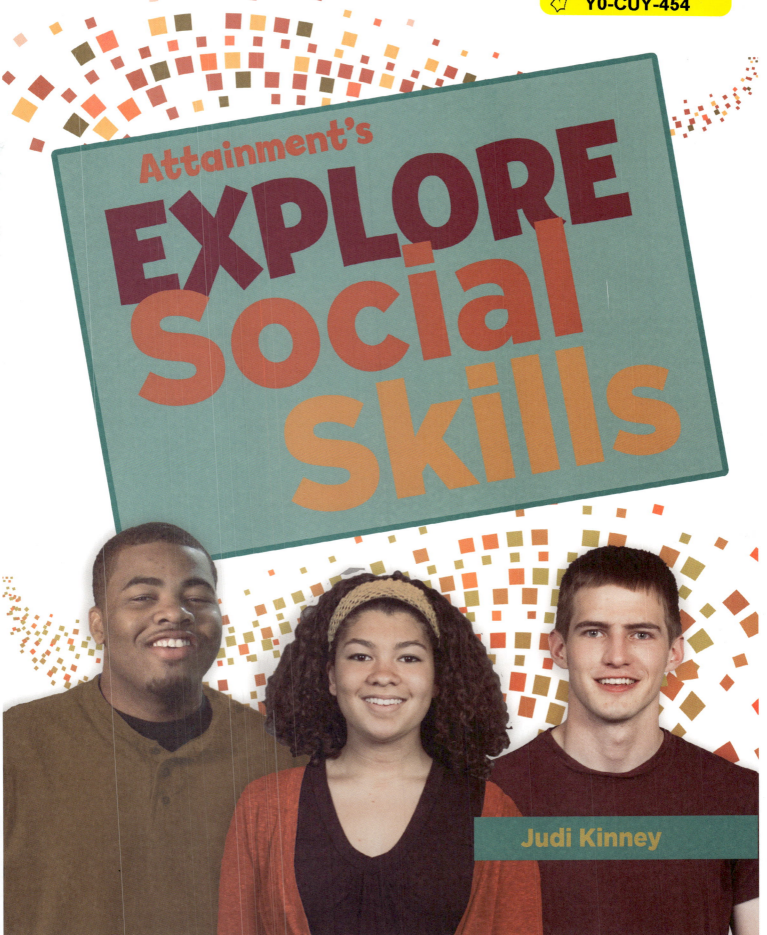

Judi Kinney

# Explore Social Skills

By Judi Kinney, MS

Edited by Tom Kinney
Graphic design by Jo Reynolds
Video stills by Jeff Schultz

An Attainment Company Publication
© 2012 Attainment Company, Inc. All rights reserved.
Printed in the United States of America

ISBN: 1-57861-806-1

**Attainment Company, Inc.**
P.O. Box 930160
Verona, Wisconsin 53593-0160 USA
1-800-327-4269
www.AttainmentCompany.com

# Table of Contents

# On the Way to School

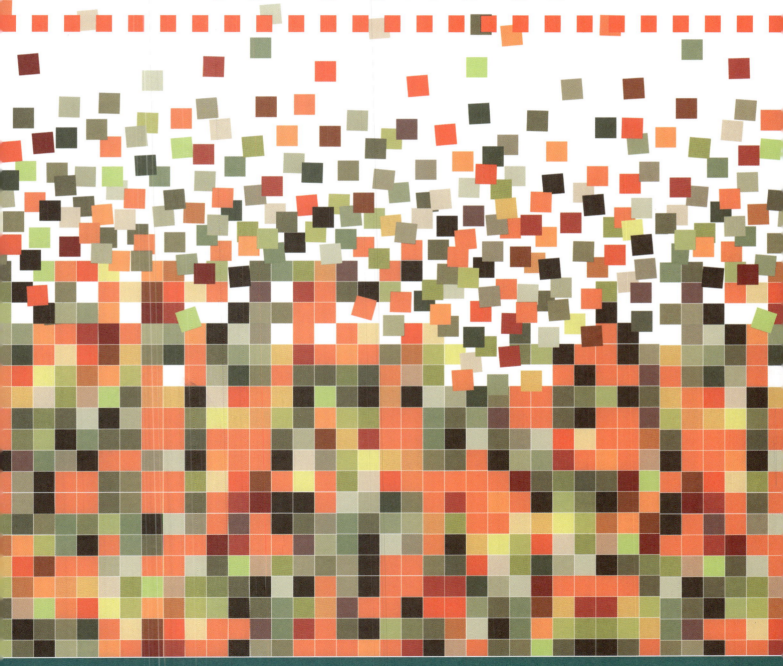

# Getting Ready for School

## self-talk story

I have trouble getting ready for school. I'm sleepy and sometimes get up late. I can't always find my homework and my teachers are unhappy with me when I leave it at home. I need to follow a plan for getting organized and being ready for school.

## steps

1  I get up when the alarm clock rings.

2  I wash, use deodorant, and brush my teeth and hair.

3  I get dressed and check myself in the mirror.

4  I eat breakfast.

5  I get all of my homework and put it in my backpack.

6  I say goodbye and leave on time.

**1** **I get up when the alarm clock rings.**

**2** **I wash, use deodorant, and brush my teeth and hair.**

**3** **I get dressed and check myself in the mirror.**

**4**

I eat breakfast.

**5**

I get all of my homework and put it in my backpack.

**6**

I say goodbye and leave on time.

# self-monitoring checklist

| M | Tu | W | Th | F | Waiting for the Bus |
|---|----|----|----|----|----|
| ☐ | ☐ | ☐ | ☐ | ☐ | 1. I get up when the alarm clock rings. |
| ☐ | ☐ | ☐ | ☐ | ☐ | 2. I wash, use deodorant, and brush my teeth and hair. |
| ☐ | ☐ | ☐ | ☐ | ☐ | 3. I get dressed and check myself in the mirror. |
| ☐ | ☐ | ☐ | ☐ | ☐ | 4. I eat breakfast. |
| ☐ | ☐ | ☐ | ☐ | ☐ | 5. I get all of my homework and put it in my backpack. |
| ☐ | ☐ | ☐ | ☐ | ☐ | 6. I say goodbye and leave on time. |

**Problem** 1. The alarm rings but you have trouble getting up and are often late. Tell one thing you can do.

**Comment** _____

_____

_____

**Problem** 2. Every morning you have trouble finding your backpack. Tell one thing you can do.

**Comment** _____

_____

_____

# Walking to School

## self-talk story

I walk to school every day. I remember to stay on the sidewalks, watch for people in front of me, and greet friends when I see them. I avoid sending text messages on my phone while walking so I can watch for people and cars. I cross the street at the crosswalks, look for cars, and stay in the crosswalks. I try to get to school as quickly as possible.

## steps

1  I stay on the sidewalks.

2  I greet my friends.

3  I look for moving cars before crossing the street.

4  I use crosswalks and traffic lights.

5  I avoid sending text messages while crossing the street.

6  I get to school before the bell rings.

**1**

I stay on the sidewalks.

**2**

I greet my friends.

**3**

I look for moving cars before crossing the street.

**4**

I use crosswalks and traffic lights.

**5**

I avoid sending text messages while crossing the street.

**6**

I get to school before the bell rings.

# self-monitoring checklist

| M | Tu | W | Th | F | **Walking to School** |
|---|----|----|----|----|----|
| ☐ | ☐ | ☐ | ☐ | ☐ | 1. I stay on the sidewalks. |
| ☐ | ☐ | ☐ | ☐ | ☐ | 2. I greet my friends. |
| ☐ | ☐ | ☐ | ☐ | ☐ | 3. I look for moving cars before crossing the street. |
| ☐ | ☐ | ☐ | ☐ | ☐ | 4. I use crosswalks and traffic lights. |
| ☐ | ☐ | ☐ | ☐ | ☐ | 5. I avoid sending text messages while crossing the street. |
| ☐ | ☐ | ☐ | ☐ | ☐ | 6. I get to school before the bell rings. |

**Problem** 1. You are walking with a friend to school. Your friend wants to cross a street when the Don't Walk signal is flashing. Tell one thing you can do.

**Comment** _____

_____

_____

**Problem** 2. You are about to cross the street and your friend sends you a text message. Tell one thing you can do.

**Comment** _____

_____

_____

# Riding the Bus

## self-talk story

I get on the bus with my backpack and ride to school following the bus rules. After I board the bus, I greet the driver and find an empty seat. I stay in my seat and talk quietly to my friends about okay things. I use ear buds if I listen to music. I get off the bus at school.

## steps

**1**  I make sure I have my backpack.

**2**  I get on the bus and greet the driver with respect.

**3**  I sit down quietly and stay in my seat.

**4**  I talk quietly to my friends about okay things.

**5**  I can listen to music.

**6**  I get off when the bus stops at school.

**1** ▪▪▪▪▪▪▪▪▪▪▪▪

I make sure I have my backpack.

**2** ▪▪▪▪▪▪▪▪▪▪▪▪

I get on the bus and greet the driver with respect.

**3** ▪▪▪▪▪▪▪▪▪▪▪▪

I sit down quietly and stay in my seat.

**4** ------------------------

I talk quietly to my friends about okay things.

**5** ------------------------

I can listen to music.

**6** ------------------------

I get off when the bus stops at school.

# self-monitoring checklist

| M | Tu | W | Th | F | **Riding the Bus** |
|---|----|----|----|----|----|
| ☐ | ☐ | ☐ | ☐ | ☐ | 1. I make sure I have my backpack. |
| ☐ | ☐ | ☐ | ☐ | ☐ | 2. I get on the bus and greet the driver with respect. |
| ☐ | ☐ | ☐ | ☐ | ☐ | 3. I sit down quietly and stay in my seat. |
| ☐ | ☐ | ☐ | ☐ | ☐ | 4. I talk quietly to my friends about okay things. |
| ☐ | ☐ | ☐ | ☐ | ☐ | 5. I can listen to music. |
| ☐ | ☐ | ☐ | ☐ | ☐ | 6. I get off when the bus stops at school. |

**Problem**  1. You want to sit at the back of the bus but students who sit there pick on people near them. Tell one thing you can do.

**Comment** _____

_____

**Problem**  2. The bus ride to school is long and you have trouble staying in your seat. Other students complain about you moving around. Tell one thing you can do.

**Comment** _____

_____

# Riding in a Car

## self-talk story

I like having a ride to school. I get into the car and buckle my seatbelt. I use this time to go over my day's schedule. I talk about okay things to the other people in the car. Sometimes sitting for a long time is hard for me. I can listen to music but I need to follow the rules and not distract the driver. I thank the driver for bringing me to school.

## steps

1  I get my backpack.

2  I decide where to sit, in the front or the back seat.

3  I buckle my seat belt.

4  I talk about okay things.

5  I don't distract the driver.

6  I thank the driver when I get to school.

**1** ----------

I get my backpack.

**2** ----------

I decide where to sit, in the front or the back seat.

**3** ----------

I buckle my seat belt.

**4**

I talk about okay things.

**5**

I don't distract the driver.

**6**

I thank the driver when I get to school.

# self-monitoring checklist

|  M | Tu |  W | Th |  F | **Riding in a Car** |
|----|----|----|----|----|---------------------|
| ☐ | ☐ | ☐ | ☐ | ☐ | 1. I get my backpack. |
| ☐ | ☐ | ☐ | ☐ | ☐ | 2. I decide where to sit, in the front or the back seat. |
| ☐ | ☐ | ☐ | ☐ | ☐ | 3. I buckle my seat belt. |
| ☐ | ☐ | ☐ | ☐ | ☐ | 4. I talk about okay things. |
| ☐ | ☐ | ☐ | ☐ | ☐ | 5. I don't distract the driver. |
| ☐ | ☐ | ☐ | ☐ | ☐ | 6. I thank the driver when I get to school. |

**Problem**  1. You and your brother like to sit in the front seat and argue over it. Tell one thing you can do.

**Comment** _____

_____

_____

**Problem**  2. The person driving you to school doesn't like your music. Tell one thing you can do.

**Comment** _____

_____

_____

# Transitions

# Walking into School

## self-talk story

I like being outside but entering school is hard for me. I try to slow down and talk softly enough to not distract others. Sometimes the noise in the halls bothers me or I walk too fast and bump into people. I try to be careful.

## steps

1   I walk into school at a normal pace.

2   I make sure my shoes are clean.

3   I greet people in a normal voice.

4   I walk around groups of people who are talking.

5   I go directly to my locker to get ready for the day.

**1** I walk into school at a normal pace.

**2** I make sure my shoes are clean.

**3** I greet people in a normal voice.

**4**

I walk around groups of people who are talking.

**5**

I go directly to my locker to get ready for the day.

# self-monitoring checklist

| M | Tu | W | Th | F | **Walking into School** |
|---|----|----|----|----|----|
| ☐ | ☐ | ☐ | ☐ | ☐ | 1. I walk into school at a normal pace. |
| ☐ | ☐ | ☐ | ☐ | ☐ | 2. I make sure my shoes are clean. |
| ☐ | ☐ | ☐ | ☐ | ☐ | 3. I greet people in a normal voice. |
| ☐ | ☐ | ☐ | ☐ | ☐ | 4. I walk around groups of people who are talking. |
| ☐ | ☐ | ☐ | ☐ | ☐ | 5. I go directly to my locker to get ready for the day. |

**Problem**   1. You are trying to get to your locker and some people are walking slowly in front of you. Tell one thing you can do.

**Comment** _____

_____

_____

**Problem**   2. When you see a friend in the hallway you stop and talk too long and are late to class. Tell one thing you can do.

**Comment** _____

_____

_____

# Organizing for Class

## self-talk story

I have trouble being organized. I make sure I have the materials I need for my classes. I check my class schedule and assignment book to be sure I have my homework to turn in. I get what I need for my next class. I make sure my cell phone is off so it won't disturb my class. I lock my locker and walk to class.

## steps

**1** I unpack my backpack.

**2** I look at my class schedule.

**3** I check my assignment book to see if I need to turn in any homework.

**4** I get all of the books and materials I need for the next class.

**5** I make sure my cell phone is turned off or is on vibration.

**6** I lock my locker and walk to class.

**1**

I unpack my backpack.

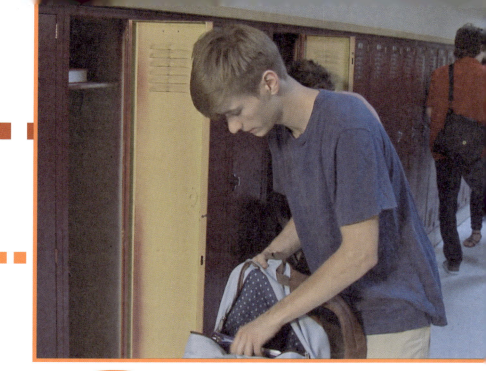

**2**

I look at my class schedule.

**3**

I check my assignment book to see if I need to turn in any homework.

**4** --------------------

I get all of the books
and materials I need
for the next class.

**5** --------------------

I make sure my
cell phone is
turned off or is
on vibration.

**6** --------------------

I lock my locker
and walk to class.

# self-monitoring checklist

| M | Tu | W | Th | F | Organizing for Class |
|---|----|----|----|----|----------------------|
| ☐ | ☐ | ☐ | ☐ | ☐ | 1. I unpack my backpack. |
| ☐ | ☐ | ☐ | ☐ | ☐ | 2. I look at my class schedule. |
| ☐ | ☐ | ☐ | ☐ | ☐ | 3. I check my assignment book to see if I need to turn in any homework. |
| ☐ | ☐ | ☐ | ☐ | ☐ | 4. I get all of the books and materials I need for the next class. |
| ☐ | ☐ | ☐ | ☐ | ☐ | 5. I make sure my cell phone is turned off or is on vibration. |
| ☐ | ☐ | ☐ | ☐ | ☐ | 6. I lock my locker and walk to class. |

**Problem** 1. You rush to get to class on time but forget to bring your homework. Tell one thing you can do.

**Comment** _____

_____

_____

**Problem** 2. You have trouble keeping your locker neat and can't find what you need for class. Tell one thing you can do.

**Comment** _____

_____

_____

# Walking in the Hallway

I check to be sure I have what I need for my next class. After I close my locker, I walk down the hallway at a normal pace. Sometimes people in the hall distract me. But if I see someone I know I say "Hi" and keep walking toward my class. I remember to get to class on time.

## steps

**1** I get everything I need for my next class.

**2** I close my locker and start walking to class.

**3** I walk down the hallway at a normal pace.

**4** I say "Hi" to people I know.

**5** I keep on walking so I am not late for class.

**6** I walk quietly into class on time and sit down.

**1** I get everything I need for my next class.

**2** I close my locker and start walking to class.

**3** I walk down the hallway at a normal pace.

**4**

I say "Hi" to people I know.

**5**

I keep on walking so I am not late for class.

**6**

I walk quietly into class on time and sit down.

# self-monitoring checklist

| M | Tu | W | Th | F | Walking in the Hallway |
|---|----|----|----|----|------------------------|
| ☐ | ☐ | ☐ | ☐ | ☐ | 1. I get everything I need for my next class. |
| ☐ | ☐ | ☐ | ☐ | ☐ | 2. I close my locker and start walking to class. |
| ☐ | ☐ | ☐ | ☐ | ☐ | 3. I walk down the hallway at a normal pace. |
| ☐ | ☐ | ☐ | ☐ | ☐ | 4. I say "Hi" to people I know. |
| ☐ | ☐ | ☐ | ☐ | ☐ | 5. I keep on walking so I am not late for class. |
| ☐ | ☐ | ☐ | ☐ | ☐ | 6. I walk quietly into class on time and sit down. |

**Problem**    1. You don't like walking crowded hallways because you bump into others and don't like being touched. Tell one thing you can do.

**Comment** _____

_____

_____

**Problem**    2. To get out of the hallway you walk too fast into class and bump into people. Tell one thing you can do.

**Comment** _____

_____

_____

# Standing in Line

When standing in line I stay in my own place. I respect others and don't let friends cut in front of me. I keep my hands and feet to myself and don't lean on others. I am patient. I don't get upset with kids in front of me if the line is slow. I talk to friends in a normal voice about class or make plans for the weekend.

## steps

1  I stay in my place.

2  I keep my hands and feet to myself.

3  I keep space between others and myself.

4  I talk in a normal voice.

5  I talk about okay things.

**1**

I stay in my place.

**2**

I keep my hands and feet to myself.

**3**

I keep space between others and myself.

**4**

I talk in a normal voice.

**5**

I talk about okay things.

# self-monitoring checklist

| M | Tu | W | Th | F | **Standing in Line** |
|---|---|---|---|---|---|
| ☐ | ☐ | ☐ | ☐ | ☐ | 1. I stay in my place. |
| ☐ | ☐ | ☐ | ☐ | ☐ | 2. I keep my hands and feet to myself. |
| ☐ | ☐ | ☐ | ☐ | ☐ | 3. I keep space between others and myself. |
| ☐ | ☐ | ☐ | ☐ | ☐ | 4. I talk in a normal voice. |
| ☐ | ☐ | ☐ | ☐ | ☐ | 5. I talk about okay things. |

**Problem**   1. It is hard for you to stand in line and respect the body space of others. Tell one thing you can do.

**Comment**   _____

_____

_____

**Problem**   2. You want to talk to others standing in line but don't know what to say. Tell one thing you can do.

**Comment**   _____

_____

_____

# Checking Out of School

## self-talk story

At the end of the school day I check my assignment notebook. I put all of the books and materials I need into my backpack. I check to be sure I have my phone and other personal items. I put on my jacket or coat. I lock my locker and walk out of the school building.

## steps

1   I check my assignment notebook.

2   I put my books and homework in my backpack.

3   I check to be sure I have all personal items and put on my coat or jacket.

4   I lock my locker.

5   I walk out of the school building.

**1** I check my assignment notebook.

**2** I put my books and homework in my backpack.

**3** I check to be sure I have all personal items and put on my coat or jacket.

**4**

I lock my locker.

**5**

I walk out of the
school building.

# self-monitoring checklist

| M | Tu | W | Th | F | Checking Out of School |
|---|----|----|----|----|---|
| ☐ | ☐ | ☐ | ☐ | ☐ | 1. I check my assignment notebook. |
| ☐ | ☐ | ☐ | ☐ | ☐ | 2. I put my books and homework in my backpack. |
| ☐ | ☐ | ☐ | ☐ | ☐ | 3. I check to be sure I have all personal items and put on my coat or jacket. |
| ☐ | ☐ | ☐ | ☐ | ☐ | 4. I lock my locker. |
| ☐ | ☐ | ☐ | ☐ | ☐ | 5. I walk out of the school building. |

**Problem** 1. You have a friend who hangs out at your locker after school and distracts you. You forget to put what you need in your backpack. Tell one thing you can do.

**Comment** _____

_____

_____

**Problem** 2. You often forget to take home all of your homework. Tell one thing you can do.

**Comment** _____

_____

_____

# Classroom

# Walking into Class

## self-talk story

Being ready for class helps me learn better. I look at my assignment notebook and get what I need for class from my locker. I walk to class and greet friends by saying "Hi." I sit down and wait for teacher directions. I talk in a normal voice until the bell rings and then I am quiet.

## steps

1  I check my assignment notebook.

2  I get books and other things I need for class.

3  I walk down the hallway.

4  I walk into class, greet friends, and sit down.

5  I talk in a normal voice to my friends.

6  I stop talking and look at the teacher when the bell rings.

**1**

I check my assignment notebook.

**2**

I get books and other things I need for class.

**3**

I walk down the hallway.

**4** ------------------------

I walk into class, greet friends, and sit down.

**5** ------------------------

I talk in a normal voice to my friends.

**6** ------------------------

I stop talking and look at the teacher when the bell rings.

# self-monitoring checklist

| M | Tu | W | Th | F | **Walking into Class** |
|---|----|----|----|----|---|
| ☐ | ☐ | ☐ | ☐ | ☐ | 1. I check my assignment notebook. |
| ☐ | ☐ | ☐ | ☐ | ☐ | 2. I get books and other things I need for class. |
| ☐ | ☐ | ☐ | ☐ | ☐ | 3. I walk down the hallway. |
| ☐ | ☐ | ☐ | ☐ | ☐ | 4. I walk into class, greet friends, and sit down. |
| ☐ | ☐ | ☐ | ☐ | ☐ | 5. I talk in a normal voice to my friends. |
| ☐ | ☐ | ☐ | ☐ | ☐ | 6. I stop talking and look at the teacher when the bell rings. |

**Problem** 1. You have a friend who keeps talking to you after a class has started. Tell one thing you can do.

**Comment** _____

_____

_____

**Problem** 2. You are constantly late to one of your classes. Tell one thing you can do.

**Comment** _____

_____

_____

# Working in a Large Group

## self-talk story

When the teacher starts talking I sit quietly and listen. When she tells the class to begin working I start my work. If I forget what I'm supposed to do I look at what other students are doing. If I need help I raise my hand. When I say something in class it is about what the teacher is discussing.

## steps

1  I stop talking when the teacher talks.

2  I start my work.

3  I watch others for what I'm supposed to do.

4  I raise my hand for questions.

5  I pay attention to my work until I'm finished.

**1** ------------

I stop talking when the teacher talks.

**2** ------------

I start my work.

**3** ------------

I watch others for what I'm supposed to do.

**4**

I raise my hand for questions.

**5**

I pay attention to my work until I'm finished.

# self-monitoring checklist

| M | Tu | W | Th | F | **Working in a Large Group** |
|---|----|----|----|----|------------------------------|
| ☐ | ☐ | ☐ | ☐ | ☐ | 1. I stop talking when the teacher talks. |
| ☐ | ☐ | ☐ | ☐ | ☐ | 2. I start my work. |
| ☐ | ☐ | ☐ | ☐ | ☐ | 3. I watch others for what I'm supposed to do. |
| ☐ | ☐ | ☐ | ☐ | ☐ | 4. I raise my hand for questions. |
| ☐ | ☐ | ☐ | ☐ | ☐ | 5. I pay attention to my work until I'm finished. |

**Problem** 1. You did not understand a direction but are too shy to raise your hand for help. Tell one thing you can do.

**Comment** _____

_____

_____

**Problem** 2. You are distracted by the movement of the other students in class when working on an assignment. Tell one thing you can do.

**Comment** _____

_____

_____

# Working in a Small Group

## self-talk story

When I work with a partner or a group I do my part. I help them plan how to do the assignment. I share pencils, books, and other materials with them. I thank them for helping me. I give at least one compliment to the group.

## steps

1  I do the assigned job.

2  I share the materials.

3  I share at least one idea.

4  I thank those who helped.

5  I compliment the people in my group.

**1**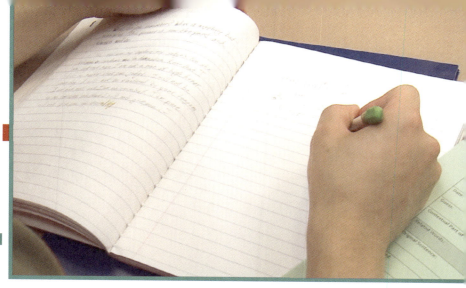

I do the assigned job.

**2**

I share the materials.

**3**

I share at least one idea.

**4**

I thank those
who helped.

**5**

I compliment
the people in my
group.

# self-monitoring checklist

| M | Tu | W | Th | F | Working in a Small Group |
|---|----|----|----|---|---|
| ☐ | ☐ | ☐ | ☐ | ☐ | 1.  I do the assigned job. |
| ☐ | ☐ | ☐ | ☐ | ☐ | 2.  I share the materials. |
| ☐ | ☐ | ☐ | ☐ | ☐ | 3.  I share at least one idea. |
| ☐ | ☐ | ☐ | ☐ | ☐ | 4.  I thank those who helped. |
| ☐ | ☐ | ☐ | ☐ | ☐ | 5.  I compliment the people in my group. |

**Problem**   1.  You are working with a group of students on a project and want to help but don't know what to do. Tell one thing you can do.

**Comment** _____

_____

_____

**Problem**   2.  You are working with students on a project and you have a good idea but are too shy to share it. Tell one thing you can do.

**Comment** _____

_____

_____

# Working in the Computer Lab

Sometimes I go to the computer lab for a class. I follow the rules and use the computers only for my work. If I need help I raise my hand. I work quietly and try to finish my work.

## steps

**1** I walk quietly into the computer lab.

**2** I find a computer I can use.

**3** I use the computer only to do my assignment.

**4** I raise my hand if I need help.

**5** I turn the computer off when I leave the lab.

**1**

I walk quietly into the computer lab.

**2**

I find a computer I can use.

**3**

I use the computer only to do my assignment.

**4**

I raise my hand if I need help.

**5**

I turn the computer off when I leave the lab.

# self-monitoring checklist

| M | Tu | W | Th | F | Working in the Computer Lab |
|---|----|---|----|---|------------------------------|
| ☐ | ☐ | ☐ | ☐ | ☐ | 1. I walk quietly into the computer lab. |
| ☐ | ☐ | ☐ | ☐ | ☐ | 2. I find a computer I can use. |
| ☐ | ☐ | ☐ | ☐ | ☐ | 3. I use the computer only to do my assignment. |
| ☐ | ☐ | ☐ | ☐ | ☐ | 4. I raise my hand if I need help. |
| ☐ | ☐ | ☐ | ☐ | ☐ | 5. I turn the computer off when I leave the lab. |

**Problem** 1. You are working in the lab and a friend wants you to join a chat room. Tell one thing you can do.

**Comment** _____

_____

_____

**Problem** 2. You are working on a project and see a video you want to download but don't know how to do it. Tell one thing you can do.

**Comment** _____

_____

_____

# Working in a Science Lab

## self-talk story

I go to lab for my science class. When I walk into the lab I put my backpack where it belongs. I follow teacher directions. I wear safety glasses and lab clothes when I'm told to. I use only the materials the teacher gives me. I clean up my area and wash my hands before I leave the lab.

## steps

1 I walk into the lab and put my belongings in an assigned place.

2 I put on my safety glasses and other lab clothing.

3 I listen to the teacher's directions.

4 I use only the materials the teacher tells me to use.

5 If I have questions I raise my hand.

6 I clean up my area and wash my hands before I leave the lab.

**1** I walk into the lab and put my belongings in an assigned place.

**2** I put on my safety glasses and other lab clothing.

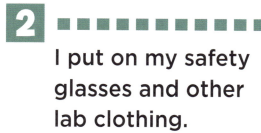

**3** I listen to the teacher's directions.

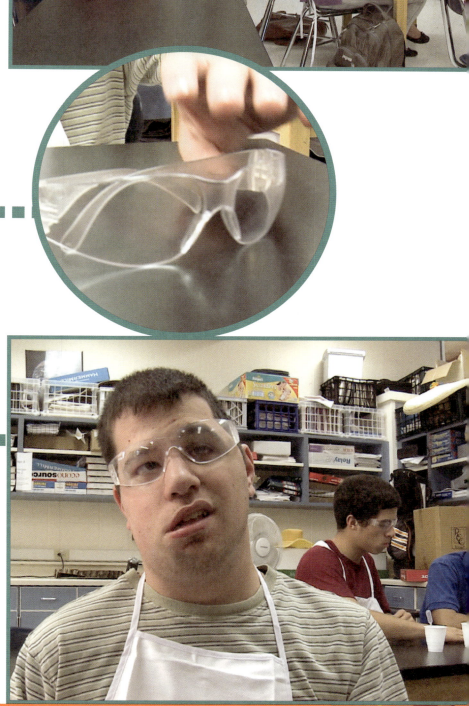

**4** ----------

I use only the materials the teacher tells me to use.

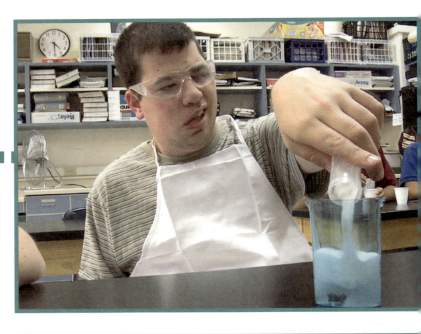

**5** ----------

If I have questions I raise my hand.

**6** ----------

I clean up my area and wash my hands before I leave the lab.

# self-monitoring checklist

| M | Tu | W | Th | F | Working in a Science Lab |
|---|----|----|----|----|--------------------------|
| ☐ | ☐ | ☐ | ☐ | ☐ | 1. I walk into the lab and put my belongings in an assigned place. |
| ☐ | ☐ | ☐ | ☐ | ☐ | 2. I put on my safety glasses and other lab clothing. |
| ☐ | ☐ | ☐ | ☐ | ☐ | 3. I listen to the teacher's directions. |
| ☐ | ☐ | ☐ | ☐ | ☐ | 4. I use only the materials the teacher tells me to use. |
| ☐ | ☐ | ☐ | ☐ | ☐ | 5. If I have questions I raise my hand. |
| ☐ | ☐ | ☐ | ☐ | ☐ | 6. I clean up my area and wash my hands before I leave the lab. |

**Problem**    1. Your science lab partner wants you to mix chemicals together to see what happens. Tell one thing you can do.

**Comment** _____

_____

_____

**Problem**    2. You missed a lab experiment because you were sick. Tell one thing you can do.

**Comment** _____

_____

_____

# Outside the Classroom

# Eating in the Cafeteria

## self-talk story

I like to eat with my friends. I remember not to talk with food in my mouth. I talk about things that are okay in school. When I finish eating I use a napkin to clean my face and hands. I clean up my area and put the trash in the correct bins. I walk out of the cafeteria.

## steps

1   I find a seat with my friends.

2   I talk about okay things.

3   I don't talk with food in my mouth.

4   I clean my hands and face with my napkin.

5   I clean up my area.

6   I put my trash in the correct bins and walk out of the cafeteria.

**1** I find a seat with my friends.

**2** I talk about okay things.

**3** I don't talk with food in my mouth.

**4**

I clean my hands and face with my napkin.

**5**

I clean up my area.

**6**

I put my trash in the correct bins and walk out of the cafeteria.

# self-monitoring checklist

| M | Tu | W | Th | F | Eating in the Cafeteria |
|---|----|---|----|---|-------------------------|
| ☐ | ☐ | ☐ | ☐ | ☐ | 1. I find a seat with my friends. |
| ☐ | ☐ | ☐ | ☐ | ☐ | 2. I talk about okay things. |
| ☐ | ☐ | ☐ | ☐ | ☐ | 3. I don't talk with food in my mouth. |
| ☐ | ☐ | ☐ | ☐ | ☐ | 4. I clean my hands and face with my napkin. |
| ☐ | ☐ | ☐ | ☐ | ☐ | 5. I clean up my area. |
| ☐ | ☐ | ☐ | ☐ | ☐ | 6. I put my trash in the correct bins and walk out of the cafeteria. |

**Problem** 1. The only seat you can find in the cafeteria is at a table of students you don't know. Tell one thing you can do.

**Comment** _____

_____

_____

**Problem** 2. You have a friend who takes food from your tray without asking. Tell one thing you can do.

**Comment** _____

_____

_____

# Emergency Drills

## self-talk story

During emergency drills I pay attention to my teacher and do not talk to my friends. After the alarm rings I listen to my teacher. I walk safely to where my teacher tells me to go. I do not push people or talk. I sit or stand quietly until the teacher tells me to go back to class. I walk back to class and sit down.

## steps

1   I hear the alarm and look at my teacher.

2   I listen to my teacher's directions.

3   I walk to the safe area.

4   I sit or stand quietly.

5   I return to class when the teacher tells me to go back.

**1** I hear the alarm and look at my teacher.

**2** I listen to my teacher's directions.

**3** I walk to the safe area.

**4**

I sit or stand quietly.

**5**

I return to class when the teacher tells me to go back.

# self-monitoring checklist

| M | Tu | W | Th | F | **Emergency Drills** |
|---|----|----|----|----|----------------------|
| ☐ | ☐ | ☐ | ☐ | ☐ | 1. I hear the alarm and look at my teacher. |
| ☐ | ☐ | ☐ | ☐ | ☐ | 2. I listen to my teacher's directions. |
| ☐ | ☐ | ☐ | ☐ | ☐ | 3. I walk to the safe area. |
| ☐ | ☐ | ☐ | ☐ | ☐ | 4. I sit or stand quietly. |
| ☐ | ☐ | ☐ | ☐ | ☐ | 5. I return to class when the teacher tells me to go back. |

**Problem**   1. The sound of the fire alarm hurts your ears and you can't hear your teacher's directions. Tell one thing you can do.

**Comment** _____

_____

_____

**Problem**   2. Tornado drills make you anxious because you're not comfortable with people kneeling close to you. Tell one thing you can do.

**Comment** _____

_____

_____

# Pep Rally

## self-talk story

When there is a pep rally I go to the gym. I sit with my friends. I talk about okay things and stop talking when the rally begins. I listen to those talking or performing. I clap when I am supposed to clap. I cheer when I am supposed to cheer. I enjoy the pep rally.

## steps

1 I walk into the gym.

2 I find a place to sit.

3 I talk to my friends about okay things.

4 I look at and listen to the people in the pep rally.

5 I clap and cheer when I am supposed to do it.

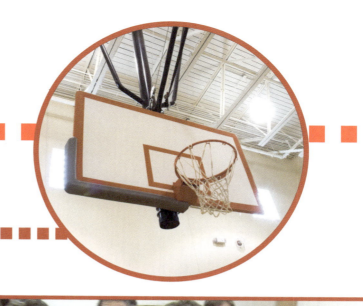

**1**

I walk into
the gym.

**2**

I find a place
to sit.

**3**

I talk to my
friends about
okay things.

**4**

I look at and listen to the people in the pep rally.

**5**

I clap and cheer when I am supposed to do it.

# self-monitoring checklist

| M | Tu | W | Th | F | Pep Rally |
|---|----|----|----|----|-----------|
| ☐ | ☐ | ☐ | ☐ | ☐ | 1. I walk into the gym. |
| ☐ | ☐ | ☐ | ☐ | ☐ | 2. I find a place to sit. |
| ☐ | ☐ | ☐ | ☐ | ☐ | 3. I talk to my friends about okay things. |
| ☐ | ☐ | ☐ | ☐ | ☐ | 4. I look at and listen to the people in the pep rally. |
| ☐ | ☐ | ☐ | ☐ | ☐ | 5. I clap and cheer when I am supposed to do it. |

**Problem** 1. Before the pep rally a student rushes by and bumps into you in a hurry to find a seat. Tell one thing you can do.

**Comment** _____

_____

_____

**Problem** 2. You get so excited at the rally that you stand up to cheer and the others ask you to sit down. Tell one thing you can do.

**Comment** _____

_____

_____

# Sports Events

## self-talk story

I like sports and watching my school's team play. When I enter the gym or stadium I find the seats where my school sits. I cheer for my team but use okay words and gestures. I can take photos of my team. I don't boo the other team or referees. I talk to friends in a normal voice. I follow all rules for my school at sporting events.

## steps

1   I sit in the seats assigned to my school.

2   I can cheer for my team.

3   I don't boo the other team or referees.

4   I can talk to my friends in a normal voice.

5   I talk about okay things and use okay language.

6   I follow school rules for sporting events.

**1** I sit in the seats assigned to my school.

**2** I can cheer for my team.

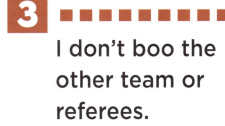

**3** I don't boo the other team or referees.

**4**

I can talk to my friends in a normal voice.

**5**

I talk about okay things and use okay language.

**6**

I follow school rules for sporting events.

# self-monitoring checklist

| M | Tu | W | Th | F | Sports Events |
|---|----|----|----|----|----|
| ☐ | ☐ | ☐ | ☐ | ☐ | 1. I sit in the seats assigned to my school. |
| ☐ | ☐ | ☐ | ☐ | ☐ | 2. I can cheer for my team. |
| ☐ | ☐ | ☐ | ☐ | ☐ | 3. I don't boo the other team or referees. |
| ☐ | ☐ | ☐ | ☐ | ☐ | 4. I can talk to my friends in a normal voice. |
| ☐ | ☐ | ☐ | ☐ | ☐ | 5. I talk about okay things and use okay language. |
| ☐ | ☐ | ☐ | ☐ | ☐ | 6. I follow school rules for sporting events. |

**Problem**   1. The home team had a ball intercepted and the home crowd is upset and starts to boo. Tell one thing you can do.

**Comment** _____

_____

_____

**Problem**   2. Students in your section start to boo and want you to join in with them. Tell one thing you can do.

**Comment** _____

_____

_____

# Peer
# Relationships

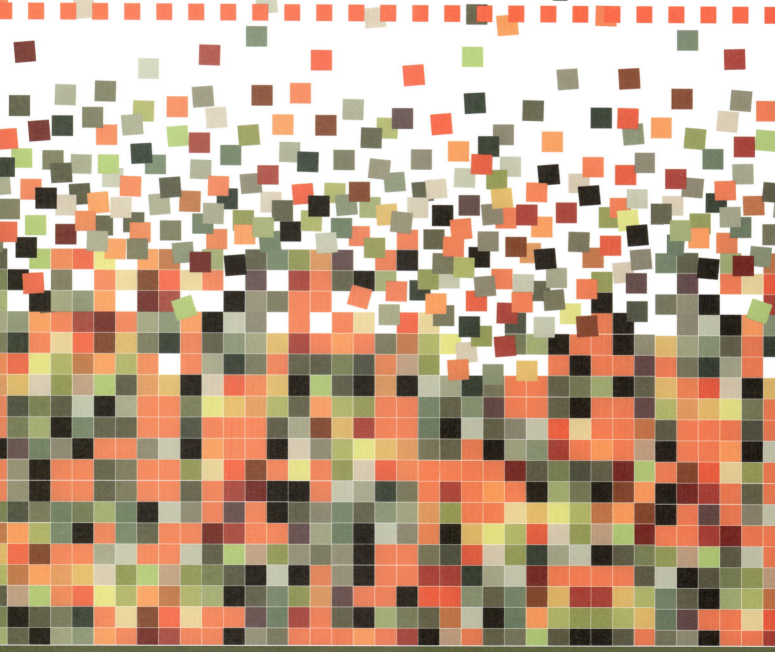

# Greeting Friends

## self-talk story

When I see a friend I say "Hi." If a friend is across the street I wave at her. When I walk up to a friend I smile and say "Hi" (and the person's name). I speak in a normal voice and look at my friend's face. I talk to my friend about school or something I did. I talk to my friend about okay things.

## steps

1   When I see a friend approach I wave.

2   I say "Hi" (and the person's name).

3   I use a normal voice.

4   I look at my friend's face.

5   I greet friends in a friendly way.

6   I talk about okay things with my friend.

**1** ············

When I see a friend approach I wave.

**2** ··············

I say "Hi" (and the person's name).

**3** ············

I use a normal voice.

**4**

I look at my friend's face.

**5**

I greet friends in a friendly way.

**6**

I talk about okay things with my friend.

# self-monitoring checklist

| M | Tu | W | Th | F | **Greeting Friends** |
|---|----|----|----|----|----------------------|
| ☐ | ☐ | ☐ | ☐ | ☐ | 1. When I see a friend approach I wave. |
| ☐ | ☐ | ☐ | ☐ | ☐ | 2. I say "Hi" (and the person's name). |
| ☐ | ☐ | ☐ | ☐ | ☐ | 3. I use a normal voice. |
| ☐ | ☐ | ☐ | ☐ | ☐ | 4. I look at my friend's face. |
| ☐ | ☐ | ☐ | ☐ | ☐ | 5. I greet friends in a friendly way. |
| ☐ | ☐ | ☐ | ☐ | ☐ | 6. I talk about okay things with my friend. |

**Problem** 1. You see a friend and want to talk but have trouble looking at people's faces. Tell one thing you can do.

**Comment** _____

_____

_____

**Problem** 2. When you see a friend you get excited and walk up too close to your friend. Tell one thing you can do.

**Comment** _____

_____

_____

# Starting a Conversation

## self-talk story

When I see someone I want to talk to, I think about what to say. I say "Hi (and his name), how are you?" I wait for him to talk before I speak again. Then I tell him what I want to say, like what I want to do with him, or what I did last night. When he talks to me, I look at his face. When it is time to go, I say, "Goodbye (and his name), I'll see you later!"

## steps

1 When I see a friend I say "Hi" (and his name).

2 I decide what to talk about with my friend.

3 I talk about what I want to say.

4 I listen and look at him when my friend talks.

5 I wait until my friend is finished talking before talking again.

6 I say "Goodbye" (and my friend's name) when we are done talking.

**1** ............

When I see a
friend I say "Hi"
(and his name).

**2** ............

I decide what to
talk about with
my friend.

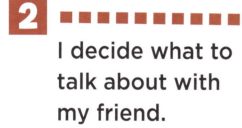

**3** ............

I talk about what
I want to say.

**4** ·············

I listen and look at him when my friend talks.

**5** ·············

I wait until my friend is finished talking before talking again.

**6** ·············

I say "Goodbye" (and my friend's name) when we are done talking.

# self-monitoring checklist

| M | Tu | W | Th | F | **Starting a Conversation** |
|---|----|----|----|---|---|
| ☐ | ☐ | ☐ | ☐ | ☐ | 1. When I see a friend I say "Hi" (and his name). |
| ☐ | ☐ | ☐ | ☐ | ☐ | 2. I decide what to talk about with my friend. |
| ☐ | ☐ | ☐ | ☐ | ☐ | 3. I talk about what I want to say. |
| ☐ | ☐ | ☐ | ☐ | ☐ | 4. I listen and look at him when my friend talks. |
| ☐ | ☐ | ☐ | ☐ | ☐ | 5. I wait until my friend is finished talking before talking again. |
| ☐ | ☐ | ☐ | ☐ | ☐ | 6. I say "Goodbye" (and my friend's name) when we are done talking. |

**Problem**  1. When you see a friend you don't know what to say. Tell one thing you can do.

**Comment** _____

_____

_____

**Problem**  2. When you see a friend you get so excited you interrupt when he is talking. Tell one thing you can do.

**Comment** _____

_____

_____

# Compromising

Sometimes my friends and I do not agree on what to do. Then, I talk to them about it and we make a new plan. The plan can have things I want to do and things they want to do. This is called compromising. I follow the plan that my friends and I made.

## steps

**1** I know why I need to compromise.

**2** I try to see the other person's side.

**3** I talk to the person about it.

**4** I help to make a plan with the other person.

**5** I follow the plan.

**1**

I know why
I need to
compromise.

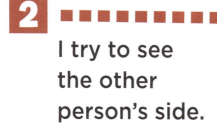

**2**

I try to see
the other
person's side.

**3**

I talk to
the person
about it.

**4**

I help to make a
plan with the
other person.

**5**

I follow the plan.

# self-monitoring checklist

| M | Tu | W | Th | F | **Compromising** |
|---|----|----|----|---|---|
| ☐ | ☐ | ☐ | ☐ | ☐ | 1. I know why I need to compromise. |
| ☐ | ☐ | ☐ | ☐ | ☐ | 2. I try to see the other person's side. |
| ☐ | ☐ | ☐ | ☐ | ☐ | 3. I talk to the person about it. |
| ☐ | ☐ | ☐ | ☐ | ☐ | 4. I help to make a plan with the other person. |
| ☐ | ☐ | ☐ | ☐ | ☐ | 5. I follow the plan. |

**Problem**    1. You need to compromise with a friend but are too angry to talk. Tell one thing you can do.

**Comment** _____

_____

_____

**Problem**    2. You made a compromise with a friend but she didn't follow the plan. Tell one thing you can do.

**Comment** _____

_____

_____

# Showing Empathy

## self-talk story

When friends are upset I can tell because they act differently. They don't smile, don't talk, and avoid others. I try to make them feel better by asking about the problem. I tell them I will listen to their concerns. I make it clear that if they don't want to talk about it that is okay. I will listen when they are ready to talk about it.

## steps

1  I know when I need to show empathy.

2  I know what it is like to be hurt and will respect my friends.

3  I ask about the problem in a calm voice.

4  I will listen carefully to what they say.

5  I know my friends may not want to talk about the problem.

6  If my friends need more time, I tell them we can talk about it later.

**1**

I know when I need to show empathy.

**2**

I know what it is like to be hurt and will respect my friends.

**3**

I ask about the problem in a calm voice.

**4**
━ ━ ━ ━ ━ ━

I will listen
carefully to what
they say.

**5**
━ ━ ━ ━ ━ ━

I know my friends
may not want to
talk about the
problem.

**6**
━ ━ ━ ━ ━ ━

If my friends
need more time,
I tell them we
can talk about
it later.

# self-monitoring checklist

|  M  | Tu  |  W  | Th  |  F  | **Showing Empathy** |
|:---:|:---:|:---:|:---:|:---:|---|
| ☐ | ☐ | ☐ | ☐ | ☐ | 1. I know when I need to show empathy. |
| ☐ | ☐ | ☐ | ☐ | ☐ | 2. I know what it is like to be hurt and will respect my friends. |
| ☐ | ☐ | ☐ | ☐ | ☐ | 3. I ask about the problem in a calm voice. |
| ☐ | ☐ | ☐ | ☐ | ☐ | 4. I will listen carefully to what they say. |
| ☐ | ☐ | ☐ | ☐ | ☐ | 5. I know my friends may not want to talk about the problem. |
| ☐ | ☐ | ☐ | ☐ | ☐ | 6. If my friends need more time, I tell them we can talk about it later. |

**Problem**  1. Your friend is feeling sad. Tell one thing you can do.

**Comment** _____

_____

_____

**Problem**  2. Your friend is feeling sad but doesn't want to talk about it. Tell one thing you can do.

**Comment** _____

_____

_____

# Responding to Teasing

## self-talk story

Sometimes at school people tease me. Teasing makes me upset and it can happen a lot. I talk to an adult about it and make a plan for when it happens. Having a plan helps me deal with it. I practice my plan and next time I'm teased I will follow it.

## steps

**1** I practice and follow a plan for when someone teases me.

**2** When it happens I stop and think if I should respond.

**3** I talk in a calm but firm voice.

**4** I can ask the person to stop teasing.

**5** I can decide to ignore the teasing.

**6** If the teasing continues I will walk away.

**1**

I practice and follow a plan for when someone teases me.

**2**

When it happens I stop and think if I should respond.

**3**

I talk in a calm but firm voice.

**4**

I can ask the person to stop teasing.

**5**

I can decide to ignore the teasing.

**6**

If the teasing continues I will walk away.

# self-monitoring checklist

| M | Tu | W | Th | F | **Responding to Teasing** |
|---|----|----|----|----|---------------------------|
| ☐ | ☐ | ☐ | ☐ | ☐ | 1. I practice and follow a plan for when someone teases me. |
| ☐ | ☐ | ☐ | ☐ | ☐ | 2. When it happens I stop and think if I should respond. |
| ☐ | ☐ | ☐ | ☐ | ☐ | 3. I talk in a calm but firm voice. |
| ☐ | ☐ | ☐ | ☐ | ☐ | 4. I can ask the person to stop teasing. |
| ☐ | ☐ | ☐ | ☐ | ☐ | 5. I can decide to ignore the teasing. |
| ☐ | ☐ | ☐ | ☐ | ☐ | 6. If the teasing continues I will walk away. |

**Problem** 1. There is a student near your locker who always teases you. Tell one thing you can do.

**Comment** _____

_____

_____

**Problem** 2. You have asked a student to stop teasing you but he hasn't gotten the message. Tell one thing you can do.

**Comment** _____

_____

_____

# Dealing with Bullies

## self-talk story

I feel uncomfortable when I see a bully. It makes me feel unsafe. I try to ignore bullies. If that doesn't work I look at the bully and use a calm but firm voice. I try to look confident and keep my body relaxed. I walk away from the bully as soon as I can. If my plan doesn't work I tell an adult about it.

## steps

1  When I see a bully I remain calm and look confident.

2  I ignore the comment.

3  If that doesn't work I use a calm but firm voice and keep my body relaxed.

4  I walk away as soon as possible.

5  I tell an adult about the bullying.

**1**

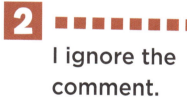

When I see a bully I remain calm and look confident.

**2**

I ignore the comment.

**3**

If that doesn't work I use a calm but firm voice and keep my body relaxed.

**4**

I walk away as soon as possible.

**5**

I tell an adult about the bullying.

# self-monitoring checklist

| M | Tu | W | Th | F | **Dealing with Bullies** |
|---|----|----|----|----|-------------------------|
| ☐ | ☐ | ☐ | ☐ | ☐ | 1. When I see a bully I remain calm and look confident. |
| ☐ | ☐ | ☐ | ☐ | ☐ | 2. I ignore the comment. |
| ☐ | ☐ | ☐ | ☐ | ☐ | 3. If that doesn't work I use a calm but firm voice and keep my body relaxed. |
| ☐ | ☐ | ☐ | ☐ | ☐ | 4. I walk away as soon as possible. |
| ☐ | ☐ | ☐ | ☐ | ☐ | 5. I tell an adult about the bullying. |

**Problem**   1. A person is bullying you on your social network. Tell one thing you can do.

**Comment** _____

_____

_____

**Problem**   2. Some bullies hang out in front of your school. They bully people who walk by them. Tell one thing you can do.

**Comment** _____

_____

_____

# Dealing with Conflict

## self-talk story

I don't want to argue with my friends. I try to avoid it but sometimes that doesn't work. Now I have a plan to resolve conflicts with my friends. I try to hear what they say and find a way to stop the argument.

## steps

1   I know what the conflict is.

2   I listen to my friend's side.

3   I talk about my side in a calm voice.

4   My friend and I brainstorm solutions to the conflict.

5   My friend and I pick a solution.

6   I try to follow the plan.

**1**

I know what the conflict is.

**2**

I listen to my friend's side.

**3**

I talk about my side in a calm voice.

**4**

My friend and I brainstorm solutions to the conflict.

**5**

My friend and I pick a solution.

**6**

I try to follow the plan.

# self-monitoring checklist

| M | Tu | W | Th | F | Dealing with Conflict |
|---|----|----|----|----|----|
| ☐ | ☐ | ☐ | ☐ | ☐ | 1. I know what the conflict is. |
| ☐ | ☐ | ☐ | ☐ | ☐ | 2. I listen to my friend's side. |
| ☐ | ☐ | ☐ | ☐ | ☐ | 3. I talk about my side in a calm voice. |
| ☐ | ☐ | ☐ | ☐ | ☐ | 4. My friend and I brainstorm solutions to the conflict. |
| ☐ | ☐ | ☐ | ☐ | ☐ | 5. My friend and I pick a solution. |
| ☐ | ☐ | ☐ | ☐ | ☐ | 6. I try to follow the plan. |

**Problem** 1. You have a conflict with a friend who blames you for a disagreement. Tell one thing you can do.

**Comment** _____

_____

_____

**Problem** 2. You have a conflict with a friend and she refuses to talk about it. Tell one thing you can do.

**Comment** _____

_____

_____

# Resisting Peer Pressure

## self-talk story

I like hanging with my friends. But sometimes they want to do things that make me uncomfortable. When this happens I stay calm and talk in a normal voice. I say "No thanks, I don't want to do that." I suggest something else to do. If my friends refuse I say "I need to go and I will talk to you later." As I walk away I think about it and if they do things that are wrong I might need new friends.

## steps

1   Sometimes my friends want to do things that make me uncomfortable.

2   I talk to them in a calm voice.

3   I say "I don't want to do that."

4   I suggest something else to do instead.

5   If my friends refuse I say "I'll talk to you later" and walk away.

6   If some friends want to do something wrong, I need to think about finding new friends.

**1**

Sometimes my friends want to do things that make me uncomfortable.

**2**

I talk to them in a calm voice.

**3**

I say "I don't want to do that."

**4**

I suggest something else to do instead.

**5**

If my friends refuse I say "I'll talk to you later" and walk away.

**6**

If some friends want to do something wrong, I need to think about finding new friends.

# self-monitoring checklist

| M | Tu | W | Th | F | **Resisting Peer Pressure** |
|---|----|----|----|----|----|
| ☐ | ☐ | ☐ | ☐ | ☐ | 1. Sometimes my friends want to do things that make me uncomfortable. |
| ☐ | ☐ | ☐ | ☐ | ☐ | 2. I talk to them in a calm voice. |
| ☐ | ☐ | ☐ | ☐ | ☐ | 3. I say "I don't want to do that." |
| ☐ | ☐ | ☐ | ☐ | ☐ | 4. I suggest something else to do instead. |
| ☐ | ☐ | ☐ | ☐ | ☐ | 5. If my friends refuse I say "I'll talk to you later" and walk away. |
| ☐ | ☐ | ☐ | ☐ | ☐ | 6. If some friends want to do something wrong I need to think about finding new friends. |

**Problem**   1. Your friend wants to skip school and says you are not cool because you don't go along with him. Tell one thing you can do.

**Comment**   _____

_____

_____

**Problem**   2. A friend is having a party and his parents will not be home. He says you have to go, everyone will be there. Tell one thing you can do.

**Comment**   _____

_____

# Resisting Pressure to Have Sex

## self-talk story

I like going places with my friends. I like group dates like movies or sport events. I like going to friends' homes. But I only go when their parents are there. Some friends want me to do things that make me uncomfortable. When this happens, I leave and join my other friends.

## steps

**1** I tell my friends I like group dates.

**2** I plan the date before going with my friends.

**3** I tell my family what I plan to do.

**4** I go to homes where there is adult supervision.

**5** I have a planned strategy to leave uncomfortable situations.

**1** I tell my friends I like group dates.

**2** I plan the date before going with my friends.

**3** I tell my family what I plan to do.

**4** --------

I go to homes where there is adult supervision.

**5** --------

I have a planned strategy to leave uncomfortable situations.

# self-monitoring checklist

| M | Tu | W | Th | F | Resisting Pressure to Have Sex |
|---|----|----|----|----|---|
| ☐ | ☐ | ☐ | ☐ | ☐ | 1. I tell my friends I like group dates. |
| ☐ | ☐ | ☐ | ☐ | ☐ | 2. I plan the date before going with my friends. |
| ☐ | ☐ | ☐ | ☐ | ☐ | 3. I tell my family what I plan to do. |
| ☐ | ☐ | ☐ | ☐ | ☐ | 4. I go to homes where there is adult supervision. |
| ☐ | ☐ | ☐ | ☐ | ☐ | 5. I have a planned strategy to leave uncomfortable situations. |

**Problem**   1.   Your friend says he wants to leave the group so he can be alone with you. Tell one thing you can do.

**Comment** _____

_____

_____

**Problem**   2.   Your girlfriend wants to come over to your house when your parents aren't home. Tell one thing you can do.

**Comment** _____

_____

_____

# Saying No

## self-talk story

I like doing things with my friends. Most of the time I have fun with them. But some friends want to do things that make me uncomfortable. I don't want to lose my friends or have them think I'm not cool, but I tell them when I don't want to do something. I say "No" when I don't want to do what they ask.

## steps

1   I look at my friends with confidence.

2   I use humor.

3   I make an excuse.

4   I suggest something else to do.

5   I say "No" using a firm voice.

6   I leave and tell my friends I will see them later.

**1**

I look at my friends with confidence.

**2**

I use humor.

**3**

I make an excuse.

**4**

I suggest something else to do.

**5**

I say "No" using a firm voice.

**6**

I leave and tell my friends I will see them later.

# self-monitoring checklist

| M | Tu | W | Th | F | Saying No |
|---|----|---|----|---|-----------|
| ☐ | ☐ | ☐ | ☐ | ☐ | 1. I look at my friends with confidence. |
| ☐ | ☐ | ☐ | ☐ | ☐ | 2. I use humor. |
| ☐ | ☐ | ☐ | ☐ | ☐ | 3. I make an excuse. |
| ☐ | ☐ | ☐ | ☐ | ☐ | 4. I suggest something else to do. |
| ☐ | ☐ | ☐ | ☐ | ☐ | 5. I say "No" using a firm voice. |
| ☐ | ☐ | ☐ | ☐ | ☐ | 6. I leave and tell my friends I will see them later. |

**Problem**    1. You told your friend you don't want to do something but he keeps pestering you. Tell one thing you can do.

**Comment** _____

_____

_____

**Problem**    2. A friend calls you names after you told her you don't want to leave school to smoke a cigarette. Tell one thing you can do.

**Comment** _____

_____

# Team Sports

# Being a Good Sport

## self-talk story

I like to play games with my friends. I practice hard and learn the rules of the game. I know it's a game and make sure everyone has a chance to play. I help other players. When someone else makes a good play I shout "Way to go!" (and their name). At the end of the game I shake the other teams' hands. I say "Thank you" when they say my team played well.

## steps

1 I learn to play well and follow the game rules.

2 I give others a chance to play.

3 I compliment players on my team.

4 I compliment players on the other team.

5 I enjoy it when I win and accept it when I lose.

**1**

I learn to play well and follow the game rules.

**2**

I give others a chance to play.

**3**

I compliment players on my team.

**4**

I compliment players on the other team.

**5**

I enjoy it when I win and accept it when I lose.

# self-monitoring checklist

| M | Tu | W | Th | F | **Being a Good Sport** |
|---|----|----|----|---|------------------------|
| ☐ | ☐ | ☐ | ☐ | ☐ | 1. I learn to play well and follow the game rules. |
| ☐ | ☐ | ☐ | ☐ | ☐ | 2. I give others a chance to play. |
| ☐ | ☐ | ☐ | ☐ | ☐ | 3. I compliment players on my team. |
| ☐ | ☐ | ☐ | ☐ | ☐ | 4. I compliment players on the other team. |
| ☐ | ☐ | ☐ | ☐ | ☐ | 5. I enjoy it when I win and accept it when I lose. |

**Problem** 1. Your team just lost a game by one point. You want to congratulate the other team. Tell one thing you can do.

**Comment** _____

_____

_____

**Problem** 2. A player on your team made a great play. Tell one thing you can do.

**Comment** _____

_____

_____

# Listening to My Coach

## self-talk story

My coach teaches us how to play. I do what coach says. When he talks I look at him and listen. I repeat back what he says so I'm sure what to do. If I have questions I ask coach. I thank coach for helping me. If coach says something I don't like, I don't argue with him. He is trying to make me a better player. Getting along with coach is part of being a good team member.

## steps

1   I have to do what my coach tells me to do.

2   I look at and listen when my coach talks to me.

3   I repeat back what my coach says.

4   If I have a question I can ask my coach.

5   I thank my coach for helping me.

**1**

I have to do what my coach tells me to do.

**2**

I look at and listen when my coach talks to me.

**3**

I repeat back what my coach says.

**4**

If I have a question I can ask my coach.

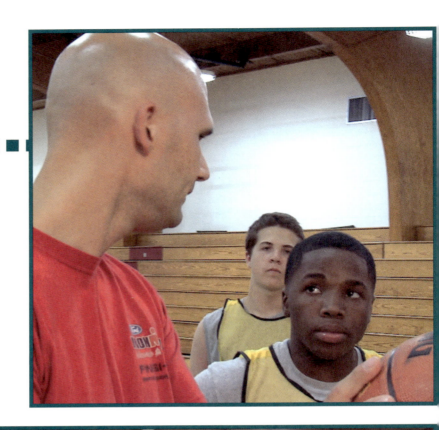

**5**

I thank my coach for helping me.

# self-monitoring checklist

| M | Tu | W | Th | F | Listening to My Coach |
|---|----|----|----|----|----|
| ☐ | ☐ | ☐ | ☐ | ☐ | 1. I have to do what my coach tells me to do. |
| ☐ | ☐ | ☐ | ☐ | ☐ | 2. I look at and listen when my coach talks to me. |
| ☐ | ☐ | ☐ | ☐ | ☐ | 3. I repeat back what my coach says. |
| ☐ | ☐ | ☐ | ☐ | ☐ | 4. If I have a question I can ask my coach. |
| ☐ | ☐ | ☐ | ☐ | ☐ | 5. I thank my coach for helping me. |

**Problem** 1. You are having trouble learning how to throw the ball to another player. Tell one thing you can do.

**Comment** _____
_____
_____

**Problem** 2. A referee makes a call you think is unfair. Tell one thing you can do.

**Comment** _____
_____
_____

# Following the Rules of the Game

## self-talk story

I have to know and follow the game rules. To learn them I listen to my coach. One rule is to wear my uniform to games. Also I learn by watching. I see how points are scored and why fouls happen. When I make a mistake I don't get angry with others. I accept the consequences. Following the rules helps me be a better teammate.

## steps

1 I wear my uniform to games.

2 I'm on time to practices and games.

3 I look at and listen to my coach.

4 I watch my teammates to see how they play the game.

5 I don't argue if I make a mistake.

**1** I wear my uniform to games.

**2** I'm on time to practices and games.

**3** I look at and listen to my coach.

**4** ----------

I watch my teammates to see how they play the game.

**5** ----------

I don't argue if I make a mistake.

# self-monitoring checklist

| M | Tu | W | Th | F | Following the Rules of the Game |
|---|----|---|----|---|----|
| ☐ | ☐ | ☐ | ☐ | ☐ | 1. I wear my uniform to games. |
| ☐ | ☐ | ☐ | ☐ | ☐ | 2. I'm on time to practices and games. |
| ☐ | ☐ | ☐ | ☐ | ☐ | 3. I look at and listen to my coach. |
| ☐ | ☐ | ☐ | ☐ | ☐ | 4. I watch my teammates to see how they play the game. |
| ☐ | ☐ | ☐ | ☐ | ☐ | 5. I don't argue if I make a mistake. |

**Problem**   1. You cannot make it to practice. Tell one thing you can do.

**Comment** _____

_____

_____

**Problem**   2. You are confused about a rule of the game. Tell one thing you can do.

**Comment** _____

_____

_____

# Important Skills

# Greeting Teachers

## self-talk story

When I see one of my teachers I don't wait for her to say "Hi." I smile and say "Hi" (and her name). I stop and talk to her if she is not busy. If I see her talking to someone, I walk around and not between them. When I go the office I say "Hi" to the secretary. I always greet adults by saying Mr., Mrs., or Ms., and their last name.

## steps

1  I look at a teacher I know.

2  I smile and greet the teacher.

3  I use Mr., Mrs., or Ms. and their last names.

4  I use first names only when adults tell me it's okay.

5  I greet other adults I know.

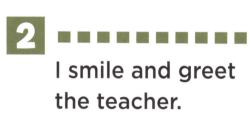

**1** I look at a teacher I know.

**2** I smile and greet the teacher.

**3** I use Mr., Mrs., or Ms. and their last names.

**4** ------------------------

I use first names
only when adults
tell me it's okay.

**5** ------------------------

I greet other
adults I know.

# self-monitoring checklist

| M | Tu | W | Th | F | Greeting Teachers |
|---|----|----|----|----|----|
| ☐ | ☐ | ☐ | ☐ | ☐ | 1. I look at a teacher I know. |
| ☐ | ☐ | ☐ | ☐ | ☐ | 2. I smile and greet the teacher. |
| ☐ | ☐ | ☐ | ☐ | ☐ | 3. I use Mr., Mrs., or Ms. and their last names. |
| ☐ | ☐ | ☐ | ☐ | ☐ | 4. I use first names only when adults tell me it's okay. |
| ☐ | ☐ | ☐ | ☐ | ☐ | 5. I greet other adults I know. |

**Problem** 1. You see a teacher you don't like in the hallway. Tell one thing you can do.

**Comment** _____

_____

_____

**Problem** 2. You are with a group of friends and see a teacher walking towards you. Tell one thing you can do.

**Comment** _____

_____

_____

# Asking for Help

## self-talk story

If I talk in class without permission it disrupts teachers and classmates. If I have a question I look at my teacher and raise my hand. I stay calm and wait for her to call on me. If my teacher calls on me I talk in a normal classroom voice.
I thank her for helping me.

## steps

1   I have a question about the assignment.

2   I look at my teacher and raise my hand.

3   I stay quiet until the teacher calls on me.

4   I use a normal tone of voice and tell her what I need.

5   I thank my teacher for helping me.

**1**

I have a question about the assignment.

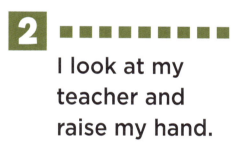

**2**

I look at my teacher and raise my hand.

**3**

I stay quiet until the teacher calls on me.

**4** ■■■■■■■■■■■■■■■■

I use a normal tone of voice and tell her what I need.

**5** ■■■■■■■■■■■■■■■■

I thank my teacher for helping me.

# self-monitoring checklist

| M | Tu | W | Th | F | **Asking for Help** |
|---|----|----|----|----|---|
| ☐ | ☐ | ☐ | ☐ | ☐ | 1. I have a question about the assignment. |
| ☐ | ☐ | ☐ | ☐ | ☐ | 2. I look at my teacher and raise my hand. |
| ☐ | ☐ | ☐ | ☐ | ☐ | 3. I stay quiet until the teacher calls on me. |
| ☐ | ☐ | ☐ | ☐ | ☐ | 4. I use a normal tone of voice and tell her what I need. |
| ☐ | ☐ | ☐ | ☐ | ☐ | 5. I thank my teacher for helping me. |

**Problem**   1. You have a question for the teacher but are afraid other students will laugh at you. Tell one thing you can do.

**Comment** _____

_____

_____

**Problem**   2. You have a question for your teacher but have trouble waiting for her to call on you. Tell one thing you can do.

**Comment** _____

_____

_____

# Making an Apology

## self-talk story

I feel bad when I hurt my friend's feelings. I still want her to be my friend and say I'm sorry for hurting her. I look at my friend and tell her "I'm sorry." I wait for my friend to say something. If she accepts my apology, we give each other high fives.

## steps

1 I ask to talk to the person.

2 I look the person in the eye.

3 I say I am sorry.

4 I wait for a response.

5 I thank the person for listening.

6 I smile and give my friend a high five.

**1**

I ask to talk to the person.

**2**

I look the person in the eye.

**3**

I say I am sorry.

**4**

I wait for a response.

**5**

I thank the person for listening.

**6**

I smile and give my friend a high five.

# self-monitoring checklist

| M | Tu | W | Th | F | **Making an Apology** |
|---|---|---|---|---|---|
| ☐ | ☐ | ☐ | ☐ | ☐ | 1. I ask to talk to the person. |
| ☐ | ☐ | ☐ | ☐ | ☐ | 2. I look the person in the eye. |
| ☐ | ☐ | ☐ | ☐ | ☐ | 3. I say I am sorry. |
| ☐ | ☐ | ☐ | ☐ | ☐ | 4. I wait for a response. |
| ☐ | ☐ | ☐ | ☐ | ☐ | 5. I thank the person for listening. |
| ☐ | ☐ | ☐ | ☐ | ☐ | 6. I smile and give my friend a high five. |

**Problem** 1. You want to apologize to your friend but he is still angry. Tell one thing you can do.

**Comment** _____

_____

_____

**Problem** 2. Your friend wants to apologize but blames you for the argument. Tell one thing you can do.

**Comment** _____

_____

_____

# Accepting Criticism

I feel frustrated and ask my friend to help me understand my feelings. What he says makes me upset but I know he is trying to help. So I listen to what he says. If I don't understand I ask him to explain again. When he is finished I thank him. Although I am angry and upset I know he told me the truth and is being honest for my sake.

## steps

1 I know when I need assistance.

2 I know when I'm wrong and can do better.

3 I recognize when advice will be helpful.

4 I keep calm when criticized.

5 I listen and say "Thank you."

**1**

I know when I need assistance.

**2**

I know when I'm wrong and can do better.

**3**

I recognize when advice will be helpful.

**4**

I keep calm when criticized.

**5**

I listen and say "Thank you."

# self-monitoring checklist

| M | Tu | W | Th | F | **Accepting Criticism** |
|---|----|----|----|----|-------------------------|
| ☐ | ☐ | ☐ | ☐ | ☐ | 1. I know when I need assistance. |
| ☐ | ☐ | ☐ | ☐ | ☐ | 2. I know when I'm wrong and can do better. |
| ☐ | ☐ | ☐ | ☐ | ☐ | 3. I recognize when advice will be helpful. |
| ☐ | ☐ | ☐ | ☐ | ☐ | 4. I keep calm when criticized. |
| ☐ | ☐ | ☐ | ☐ | ☐ | 5. I listen and say "Thank you." |

**Problem**   1. Your teacher criticizes a project you worked hard on. Tell one thing you can do.

**Comment** _____

_____

_____

**Problem**   2. Your friend criticized you and you feel angry. Tell one thing you can do.

**Comment** _____

_____

_____

# Saying Please and Thank You

## self-talk story

I thank others when they do something for me. I say "Please" when I want something, like "Please lend me a pencil." Or when I ask a favor of someone. After I get what I want I say "Thank you" and the person's name. Other people like it when I am polite.

## steps

1 When I need help or want something, I look at the person before I talk.

2 I say "Please" and what I want.

3 After the person helps me I say "Thank you" (and the person's name).

4 I smile at the person to show I am happy to have help.

5 Other people like it when I'm polite.

**1** 

When I need help or want something, I look at the person before I talk.

**2** 

I say "Please" and what I want.

**3** 

After the person helps me I say "Thank you" (and the person's name).

**4** ▪▪▪▪▪▪▪▪▪▪▪▪

I smile at the person to show I am happy to have help.

**5** ▪▪▪▪▪▪▪▪▪▪▪▪▪▪▪

Other people like it when I'm polite.

# self-monitoring checklist

| M | Tu | W | Th | F | **Saying Please and Thank You** |
|---|----|----|----|---|---|
| ☐ | ☐ | ☐ | ☐ | ☐ | 1. When I need help or want something, I look at the person before I talk. |
| ☐ | ☐ | ☐ | ☐ | ☐ | 2. I say "Please" and what I want. |
| ☐ | ☐ | ☐ | ☐ | ☐ | 3. After the person helps me I say "Thank you" (and the person's name). |
| ☐ | ☐ | ☐ | ☐ | ☐ | 4. I smile at the person to show I am happy to have help. |
| ☐ | ☐ | ☐ | ☐ | ☐ | 5. Other people like it when I'm polite. |

**Problem**   1. You want to borrow a friend's book in study hall to finish an assignment. Tell one thing you can do.

**Comment** _____

_____

_____


**Problem**   2. You have to ask for help from your teacher. Tell one thing you can do.

**Comment** _____

_____

_____

# Following Directions

## self-talk story

I need to listen to adults when I am given a direction. When my teacher tells the class to listen I stop what I'm doing and look at her. I wait until she is done before I raise my hand to ask a question. When I can't remember I watch my classmates. I copy what they are doing. I am proud when I follow directions and get assignments done right.

## steps

**1**   I stop what I am doing when the teacher talks.

**2**   I look at her and listen to her directions.

**3**   I look to see if there are written directions as well.

**4**   I watch how others do it.

**5**   If I don't understand I ask for help.

**6**   I thank my teacher for helping me.

**1** ----------------

I stop what I am
doing when the
teacher talks.

**2** ----------------

I look at her
and listen to her
directions.

**3** ----------------

I look to see if
there are written
directions as well.

**4**

I watch how others do it.

**5**

If I don't understand I ask for help.

**6**

I thank my teacher for helping me.

# self-monitoring checklist

| M | Tu | W | Th | F | **Following Directions** |
|---|----|----|----|----|----|
| ☐ | ☐ | ☐ | ☐ | ☐ | 1. I stop what I am doing when the teacher talks. |
| ☐ | ☐ | ☐ | ☐ | ☐ | 2. I look at her and listen to her directions. |
| ☐ | ☐ | ☐ | ☐ | ☐ | 3. I look to see if there are written directions as well. |
| ☐ | ☐ | ☐ | ☐ | ☐ | 4. I watch how others do it. |
| ☐ | ☐ | ☐ | ☐ | ☐ | 5. If I don't understand I ask for help. |
| ☐ | ☐ | ☐ | ☐ | ☐ | 6. I thank my teacher for helping me. |

**Problem** 1. You were daydreaming when your teacher gave directions. Tell one thing you can do.

**Comment** _____

_____

_____

**Problem** 2. You started an assignment in class but forgot what you had to do to finish it. Tell one thing you can do.

**Comment** _____

_____

_____

# Accepting Others

I don't like it when others make fun of me. It hurts my feelings. I want to keep my friends and I don't want to hurt them because it makes them unhappy. I will compliment others and say things that won't hurt them. I will avoid put-downs and accept others, even those who are different from me.

## steps

**1** I use a normal voice when talking to other people.

**2** I compliment others and avoid saying embarrassing things to them.

**3** I include others in work groups or conversations.

**4** I know that put-downs hurt people's feelings.

**5** I accept others, even people who are different.

**1** .......................................

I use a normal voice when talking to other people.

**2** .......................................

I compliment others and avoid saying embarrassing things to them.

**3** .......................................

I include others in work groups or conversations.

**4**

I know that put-downs hurt people's feelings.

**5**

I accept others, even people who are different.

# self-monitoring checklist

| M | Tu | W | Th | F | **Accepting Others** |
|---|----|----|----|----|----|
| ☐ | ☐ | ☐ | ☐ | ☐ | 1. I use a normal voice when talking to other people. |
| ☐ | ☐ | ☐ | ☐ | ☐ | 2. I compliment others and avoid saying embarrassing things to them. |
| ☐ | ☐ | ☐ | ☐ | ☐ | 3. I include others in work groups or conversations. |
| ☐ | ☐ | ☐ | ☐ | ☐ | 4. I know that put-downs hurt people's feelings. |
| ☐ | ☐ | ☐ | ☐ | ☐ | 5. I accept others, even people who are different. |

**Problem**   1. You sit next to a student who others think is very different and don't talk to her. Tell one thing you can do.

**Comment** _____

_____

_____

**Problem**   2. Your friend makes fun of a student who she thinks is very different from you. Tell one thing you can do.

**Comment** _____

_____

_____

# Accepting Compliments

## self-talk story

When I do something well friends and teachers tell me so. When they say something nice about me it's called a compliment. I remember to look at and thank them. If someone helps me on a project I give them credit.

## steps

1   I look at the person and smile.

2   I speak in a normal voice.

3   I say "Thank you" (and the person's name).

4   I say "I tried to do a good job. Thank you for noticing."

5   When someone helps me I say her name.

**1**

I look at the
person and smile.

**2**

I speak in a
normal voice.

**3**

I say "Thank you"
(and the person's
name).

**4**

I can say, "I tried to do a good job. Thank you for noticing."

**5**

When someone helps me I say her name.

# self-monitoring checklist

| M | Tu | W | Th | F | Accepting Compliments |
|---|----|----|----|----|---|
| ☐ | ☐ | ☐ | ☐ | ☐ | 1. I look at the person and smile. |
| ☐ | ☐ | ☐ | ☐ | ☐ | 2. I speak in a normal voice. |
| ☐ | ☐ | ☐ | ☐ | ☐ | 3. I say "Thank you" (and the person's name). |
| ☐ | ☐ | ☐ | ☐ | ☐ | 4. I say "I tried to do a good job. Thank you for noticing." |
| ☐ | ☐ | ☐ | ☐ | ☐ | 5. When someone helps me I say her name. |

**Problem** 1. Your teacher compliments you in front of the class. Tell one thing you can do.

**Comment** _____

_____

_____

**Problem** 2. You feel embarrassed when your friend compliments you. Tell one thing you can do.

**Comment** _____

_____

_____

# Public Places

# Eating in a Restaurant

I like to eat in restaurants with family and friends. I put my napkin on my lap and look at the menu and then order. I talk in a normal voice to those at my table. I eat my food and remember not to talk when there is food in my mouth. I ask for the bill, pay it, and leave a tip for the server.

## steps

1  I look at the menu and order my food.

2  I talk in a normal voice to the people at my table.

3  I put my napkin in my lap.

4  I remember not to talk with food in my mouth.

5  I ask for the bill and pay it.

6  I leave a tip for the server.

**1** I look at the menu and order my food.

**2** I talk in a normal voice to the people at my table.

**3** I put my napkin in my lap.

**4**

I remember not to talk with food in my mouth.

**5**

I ask for the bill and pay it.

**6**

I leave a tip for the server.

# self-monitoring checklist

| M | Tu | W | Th | F | **Eating in a Restaurant** |
|---|----|----|----|----|----|
| ☐ | ☐ | ☐ | ☐ | ☐ | 1. I look at the menu and order my food. |
| ☐ | ☐ | ☐ | ☐ | ☐ | 2. I talk in a normal voice to the people at my table. |
| ☐ | ☐ | ☐ | ☐ | ☐ | 3. I put my napkin in my lap. |
| ☐ | ☐ | ☐ | ☐ | ☐ | 4. I remember not to talk with food in my mouth. |
| ☐ | ☐ | ☐ | ☐ | ☐ | 5. I ask for the bill and pay it. |
| ☐ | ☐ | ☐ | ☐ | ☐ | 6. I leave a tip for the server. |

**Problem**    1. You're sitting in a restaurant talking to your friends and your cell phone rings. Tell one thing you can do.

**Comment** _____

_____

_____

**Problem**    2. You pay your bill using a debit card and want to leave a tip but don't know how to do it. Tell one thing you can do.

**Comment** _____

_____

_____

# Eating in a Fast Food Restaurant

## self-talk story

I like fast food restaurants and go with my friends. Standing in line I look at the menu and decide what I want. When I get my order I thank the server. I pay for my food and get napkins and other supplies. I walk to a table and talk in a normal voice with friends while I eat. I pick up after myself when I am done and throw the trash away before I leave.

## steps

1   I look at the menu and decide what to eat.

2   I order and pay for my food.

3   I thank the person behind the counter.

4   I get my napkin and other supplies.

5   I sit down and talk in a normal voice to my friends as I eat.

6   I clean up after myself and throw the trash away.

**1**

I look at the menu and decide what to eat.

**2**

I order and pay for my food.

**3**

I thank the person behind the counter.

**4** I get my napkin and other supplies.

**5** I sit down and talk in a normal voice to my friends as I eat.

**6** I clean up after myself and throw the trash away.

# self-monitoring checklist

| M | Tu | W | Th | F | **Eating in a Fast Food Restaurant** |
|---|----|---|----|----|---|
| ☐ | ☐ | ☐ | ☐ | ☐ | 1. I look at the menu and decide what to eat. |
| ☐ | ☐ | ☐ | ☐ | ☐ | 2. I order and pay for my food. |
| ☐ | ☐ | ☐ | ☐ | ☐ | 3. I thank the person behind the counter. |
| ☐ | ☐ | ☐ | ☐ | ☐ | 4. I get my napkin and other supplies. |
| ☐ | ☐ | ☐ | ☐ | ☐ | 5. I sit down and talk in a normal voice to my friends as I eat. |
| ☐ | ☐ | ☐ | ☐ | ☐ | 6. I clean up after myself and throw the trash away. |

**Problem**  1. It is your turn to order but you still don't know what you want to eat. Tell one thing you can do.

**Comment** _____

_____

_____

**Problem**  2. You are eating with your friend and he is talking to someone else on his cell phone. Tell one thing you can do.

**Comment** _____

_____

_____ w

# Laundromat

## self-talk story

I go to the Laundromat to wash and dry my clothes. I look for empty washing machines and put my clothes and detergent in the washers. While my clothes are washing I read or listen to music. If I use my cell phone I talk in a low voice so I do not distract others. When my clothes are washed, I put them in the dryer. When they are dry I fold them and leave.

## steps

1 I separate my clothes by color.

2 I find empty washers and put my clothes in the machines.

3 I select the cycle and put my money in the washers.

4 I find something quiet to do while my clothes are washing.

5 I put my clothes in the dryers and select the cycle.

6 I fold my clothes and leave the Laundromat.

**1** ..................

I separate my clothes by color.

**2** ..................

I find empty washers and put my clothes in the machines.

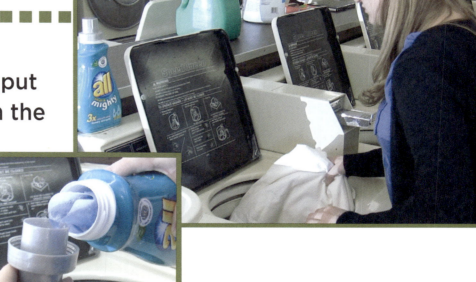

**3** ..................

I select the cycle and put my money in the washers.

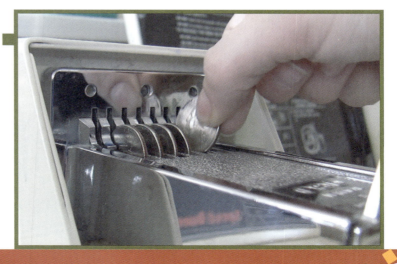

**4**

I find something quiet to do while my clothes are washing.

**5**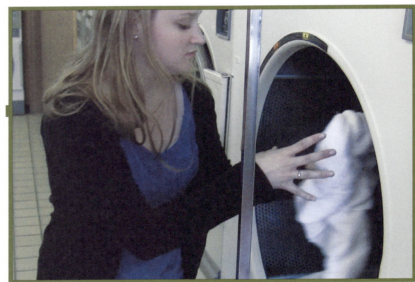

I put my clothes in the dryers and select the cycle.

**6**

I fold my clothes and leave the Laundromat.

# self-monitoring checklist

| M | Tu | W | Th | F | **Laundromat** |
|---|----|----|----|----|----------------|
| ☐ | ☐ | ☐ | ☐ | ☐ | 1. I separate my clothes by color. |
| ☐ | ☐ | ☐ | ☐ | ☐ | 2. I find empty washers and put my clothes in the machines. |
| ☐ | ☐ | ☐ | ☐ | ☐ | 3. I select the cycle and put my money in the washers. |
| ☐ | ☐ | ☐ | ☐ | ☐ | 4. I find something quiet to do while my clothes are washing. |
| ☐ | ☐ | ☐ | ☐ | ☐ | 5. I put my clothes in the dryers and select the cycle. |
| ☐ | ☐ | ☐ | ☐ | ☐ | 6. I fold my clothes and leave the Laundromat. |

**Problem** 1. You return to the Laundromat and find a customer taking your clean clothes out of a washing machine. Tell one thing you can do.

**Comment** _____

_____

_____

**Problem** 2. You have thirty minutes to wait for your clothes to dry. Tell one thing you can do.

**Comment** _____

_____

# Tech Devices

# Using Cell Phones

I use my cell phone to talk to friends and family. When I answer I talk in a normal voice. I use okay language and only say nice things about others. When I am talking to a friend and my phone rings, I ask if it is okay to answer it. I turn it off when I see a No Cell Phones sign. I turn it off in public places like school, movie theaters, airplanes, or concerts.

## steps

**1** I use my cell phone to talk to friends and family.

**2** I talk on my phone in a normal voice.

**3** I talk about okay things.

**4** If I am talking with others I ask if it is okay to answer my phone.

**5** I don't use my phone in places where cell phones aren't allowed.

**1** ........

I use my cell phone to talk to friends and family.

**2** ...........

I talk on my phone in a normal voice.

**3** ..........

I talk about okay things.

**4**

If I am talking with others I ask if it is okay to answer my phone.

**5**

I don't use my phone in places where cell phones aren't allowed.

# self-monitoring checklist

| M | Tu | W | Th | F | **Using Cell Phones** |
|---|----|----|----|----|---|
| ☐ | ☐ | ☐ | ☐ | ☐ | 1. I use my cell phone to talk to friends and family. |
| ☐ | ☐ | ☐ | ☐ | ☐ | 2. I talk on my phone in a normal voice. |
| ☐ | ☐ | ☐ | ☐ | ☐ | 3. I talk about okay things. |
| ☐ | ☐ | ☐ | ☐ | ☐ | 4. If I am talking with others I ask if it is okay to answer my phone. |
| ☐ | ☐ | ☐ | ☐ | ☐ | 5. I don't use my phone in places where cell phones aren't allowed. |

**Problem** 1. You are driving a car and your cell phone rings. Tell one thing you can do.

**Comment** _____

_____

_____

**Problem** 2. You are talking to a friend and your cell phone rings. Tell one thing you can do.

**Comment** _____

_____

_____

# Text Messages

I use my cell phone to text messages to family and friends. I use okay words. When talking on the phone would disturb others I use text messages. When I am in a public library I don't want to disturb others. When talking to another person I ask if I can text before doing it. I do not send messages where cell phone use is not allowed, like on airplanes or in movie theaters.

## steps

**1**  I text messages to my family and friends.

**2**  I use okay words.

**3**  When talking to someone else I ask if I can text a message.

**4**  I text messages in places where it would disturb people if I talked on my phone.

**5**  I don't text messages where cell phones aren't allowed.

**1**

I text messages to my family and friends.

**2**

I use okay words.

**3**

When talking to someone else I ask if I can text a message.

**4** ■■■■■■■■■■■■■■■■

I text messages in places where it would disturb people if I talked on my phone.

**5** ■■■■■■■■■■■■■■■■

I don't text messages where cell phones aren't allowed.

# self-monitoring checklist

| M | Tu | W | Th | F | Text Messages |
|---|----|----|----|----|---------------|
| ☐ | ☐ | ☐ | ☐ | ☐ | 1. I text messages to my family and friends. |
| ☐ | ☐ | ☐ | ☐ | ☐ | 2. I use okay words. |
| ☐ | ☐ | ☐ | ☐ | ☐ | 3. When talking to someone else I ask if I can text a message. |
| ☐ | ☐ | ☐ | ☐ | ☐ | 4. I text messages in places where it would disturb people if I talked on my phone. |
| ☐ | ☐ | ☐ | ☐ | ☐ | 5. I don't text messages where cell phones aren't allowed. |

**Problem**   1. A bully keeps sending you threatening text messages. Tell one thing you can do.

**Comment** _____

_____

_____

**Problem**   2. You are eating dinner with your family and a friend keeps trying to send you text messages. Tell one thing you can do.

**Comment** _____

_____

_____

# Cell Phone Photos

I use my cell phone to take photos of friends and family. I take photos of my school's teams, my pets, and on vacation. I take photos of okay things and send them to family and friends. I don't take photos that embarrass anyone. Taking and sharing photos is fun.

## steps

1   I use my cell phone to take photos.

2   I take photos of okay things.

3   I ask if I can take a photo of my family or friends.

4   I ask if I can share the photos with my family or friends.

5   I don't take photos that would embarrass my family, friends, or myself.

**1**

I use my cell phone to take photos.

**2**

I take photos of okay things.

**3**

I ask if I can take a photo of my family or friends.

**4** ----------------

I ask if I can share the photos with my family or friends.

**5** ----------------

I don't take photos that would embarrass my family, friends, or myself.

# self-monitoring checklist

| M | Tu | W | Th | F | **Cell Phone Photos** |
|---|----|----|----|---|---|
| ☐ | ☐ | ☐ | ☐ | ☐ | 1. I use my cell phone to take photos. |
| ☐ | ☐ | ☐ | ☐ | ☐ | 2. I take photos of okay things. |
| ☐ | ☐ | ☐ | ☐ | ☐ | 3. I ask if I can take a photo of my family or friends. |
| ☐ | ☐ | ☐ | ☐ | ☐ | 4. I ask if I can share the photos with my family or friends. |
| ☐ | ☐ | ☐ | ☐ | ☐ | 5. I don't take photos that would embarrass my family, friends, or myself. |

**Problem**   1. A friend is trying to get you take a photo that might embarrass you. Tell one thing you can do.

**Comment**   _____

_____

_____

**Problem**   2. A friend sends you a photo that is not okay. Tell one thing you can do.

**Comment**   _____

_____

_____

_____

# Internet Etiquette

## self-talk story

I use the Internet to find information for my classes. I follow school rules for using the Internet. I am polite to others in my emails. I don't give out personal information unless my teachers tell me it's okay. If I see something that makes me uncomfortable I tell my teachers. The Internet helps me in many ways if I use it correctly.

## steps

1. I know and follow school rules for using the Internet.

2. I search for topics the teacher tells me I need.

3. I am polite and use appropriate words in letters or emails.

4. I don't give out personal information unless okayed by an adult.

5. I tell an adult if something makes me uncomfortable.

**1**

I know and follow school rules for using the Internet.

**2**

I search for topics the teacher tells me I need.

**3**

I am polite and use appropriate words in letters or emails.

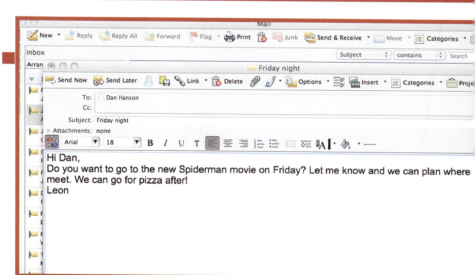

**4** ·············

I don't give
out personal
information unless
okayed
by an adult.

**5** ·············

I tell an adult if
something makes
me uncomfortable.

# self-monitoring checklist

| M | Tu | W | Th | F | Internet Etiquette |
|---|----|----|----|---|---|
| ☐ | ☐ | ☐ | ☐ | ☐ | 1. I know and follow school rules for using the Internet. |
| ☐ | ☐ | ☐ | ☐ | ☐ | 2. I search for topics the teacher tells me I need. |
| ☐ | ☐ | ☐ | ☐ | ☐ | 3. I am polite and use appropriate words in letters or emails. |
| ☐ | ☐ | ☐ | ☐ | ☐ | 4. I don't give out personal information unless okayed by an adult. |
| ☐ | ☐ | ☐ | ☐ | ☐ | 5. I tell an adult if something makes me uncomfortable. |

**Problem**   1.   You see a video that might help you with an assignment but are not sure you can download it. Tell one thing you can do.

**Comment** _____

_____

_____


**Problem**   2.   You need to send an email to your Senator but are not sure how to write it. Tell one thing you can do.

**Comment** _____

_____

_____

# Vocational Skills

# Getting Ready for Work

I follow a plan to get to work on time. I wash my face and hands, comb my hair, and brush my teeth. I wear clothes that are okay for work. I check myself in the mirror to be sure I look good. I check the time so I am not late. If I need to, I pack a snack or a meal to take with me. I leave on time so I won't be late to work.

## steps

1  I wash my hands and face, brush my teeth, and comb my hair.

2  I put on clothes that are okay for working at my job.

3  I check myself in the mirror.

4  I pack my snack or a meal.

5  I check to be sure I have change or tokens.

6  I leave on time for work.

**1** ......................

I wash my hands and face, brush my teeth, and comb my hair.

**2** ......................

I put on clothes that are okay for working at my job.

**3** ......................

I check myself in the mirror.

**4**

I pack my snack or
a meal.

**5**

I check to be sure
I have change or
tokens.

**6**

I leave on time
for work.

# self-monitoring checklist

| M | Tu | W | Th | F | **Getting Ready for Work** |
|---|----|----|----|----|-----|
| ☐ | ☐ | ☐ | ☐ | ☐ | 1. I wash my hands and face, brush my teeth, and comb my hair. |
| ☐ | ☐ | ☐ | ☐ | ☐ | 2. I put on clothes that are okay for working at my job. |
| ☐ | ☐ | ☐ | ☐ | ☐ | 3. I check myself in the mirror. |
| ☐ | ☐ | ☐ | ☐ | ☐ | 4. I pack my snack or a meal. |
| ☐ | ☐ | ☐ | ☐ | ☐ | 5. I check to be sure I have change or tokens. |
| ☐ | ☐ | ☐ | ☐ | ☐ | 6. I leave on time for work. |

**Problem** 1. You see a video that might help you with an assignment but are not sure you can download it. Tell one thing you can do.

**Comment** _____

_____

_____

**Problem** 2. You need to send an email to your Senator but are not sure how to write it. Tell one thing you can do.

**Comment** _____

_____

# Talking to My Supervisor

My supervisor tells me what to do and I do things by his rules. I like it when he gives me compliments about my work. I say "Thank you" (and my supervisor's name). When he gives me a direction I look at him and listen. I repeat what he says. I ask questions if I don't understand. I thank my supervisor for helping me.

## steps

1 I do my work according to rules my supervisor tells me.

2 I say "Thank you" (and my supervisor's name) when he gives me a compliment.

3 I look at and listen when my supervisor gives me a direction.

4 I repeat the direction to be sure I understand.

5 I ask questions if I don't understand.

6 I thank my supervisor for helping me.

**1**

I do my work according to rules my supervisor tells me.

**2**

I say "Thank you" (and my supervisor's name) when he gives me a compliment.

**3**

I look at and listen when my supervisor gives me a direction.

**4**

I repeat the direction to be sure I understand.

**5**

I ask questions if I don't understand.

**6**

I thank my supervisor for helping me.

# self-monitoring checklist

| M | Tu | W | Th | F | **Talking to My Supervisor** |
|---|----|----|----|----|---|
| ☐ | ☐ | ☐ | ☐ | ☐ | 1. I do my work according to rules my supervisor tells me. |
| ☐ | ☐ | ☐ | ☐ | ☐ | 2. I say "Thank you" (and my supervisor's name) when he gives me a compliment. |
| ☐ | ☐ | ☐ | ☐ | ☐ | 3. I look at and listen when my supervisor gives me a direction. |
| ☐ | ☐ | ☐ | ☐ | ☐ | 4. I repeat the direction to be sure I understand. |
| ☐ | ☐ | ☐ | ☐ | ☐ | 5. I ask questions if I don't understand. |
| ☐ | ☐ | ☐ | ☐ | ☐ | 6. I thank my supervisor for helping me. |

**Problem** 1. You have a new supervisor who tells you to do your job differently than the way you usually do it. Tell one thing you can do.

**Comment** _____

_____

_____

**Problem** 2. Your supervisor criticized the way you did something and it makes you angry. Tell one thing you can do.

**Comment** _____

_____

# Paying Attention to My Work

## self-talk story

I feel good when I have done my job well. I pay attention and follow the rules. I work quietly so I don't distract coworkers or supervisors. I pay attention to my work and not those around me. I finish everything I am supposed to do. I work hard and do a good job.

## steps

**1** When working I follow the rules.

**2** I work quietly so I don't distract coworkers.

**3** I focus on my work and not the people around me.

**4** I finish everything I am supposed to do.

**5** I feel happy when I have done a good job.

**1** • • • • • • • • • • • • • • •

When working I
follow the rules.

**2** • • • • • • • • • • • • • • •

I work quietly so
I don't distract
coworkers.

**3** • • • • • • • • • • • • • • •

I focus on my
work and not
the people
around me.

**4**

I finish everything I am supposed to do.

**5**

I feel happy when I have done a good job.

# self-monitoring checklist

| M | Tu | W | Th | F | Paying Attention to My Work |
|---|----|----|----|----|----|
| ☐ | ☐ | ☐ | ☐ | ☐ | 1. When working I follow the rules. |
| ☐ | ☐ | ☐ | ☐ | ☐ | 2. I work quietly so I don't distract coworkers. |
| ☐ | ☐ | ☐ | ☐ | ☐ | 3. I focus on my work and not the people around me. |
| ☐ | ☐ | ☐ | ☐ | ☐ | 4. I finish everything I am supposed to do. |
| ☐ | ☐ | ☐ | ☐ | ☐ | 5. I feel happy when I have done a good job. |

**Problem**   1. You work with a coworker you like but she interrupts your work to talk to you. Tell one thing you can do.

**Comment** _____

_____

_____

**Problem**   2. You have trouble remembering everything your supervisor told you to do to finish your work. Tell one thing you can do.

**Comment** _____

_____

_____

# Safety Rules at Work

At work I follow safety rules. I put my backpack where it belongs. I only use my cell phone on break. I know where the fire alarms are. I know how to lift heavy boxes. I keep my work area clean and make sure nothing is on the floor. I use equipment correctly and wear protective clothing if I have to. When I follow the rules it keeps my workplace safe.

## steps

1. I follow the safety rules at work.

2. I know where the fire and smoke alarms and exits are.

3. I know how to lift heavy objects.

4. I keep my work area clean and make sure that there is nothing on the floor.

5. I know the rules for using the equipment correctly.

6. If I need to, I wear protective clothing.

**1** 

I follow the safety rules at work.

**2** 

I know where the fire and smoke alarms and exits are.

**3** 

I know how to lift heavy objects.

**4**

I keep my work area clean and make sure that there is nothing on the floor.

**5**

I know the rules for using the equipment correctly.

**6**

If I need to, I wear protective clothing.

# self-monitoring checklist

| M | Tu | W | Th | F | Safety Rules at Work |
|---|----|----|----|----|---|
| ☐ | ☐ | ☐ | ☐ | ☐ | 1. I follow the safety rules at work. |
| ☐ | ☐ | ☐ | ☐ | ☐ | 2. I know where the fire and smoke alarms and exits are. |
| ☐ | ☐ | ☐ | ☐ | ☐ | 3. I know how to lift heavy objects. |
| ☐ | ☐ | ☐ | ☐ | ☐ | 4. I keep my work area clean and make sure that there is nothing on the floor. |
| ☐ | ☐ | ☐ | ☐ | ☐ | 5. I know the rules for using the equipment correctly. |
| ☐ | ☐ | ☐ | ☐ | ☐ | 6. If I need to, I wear protective clothing. |

**Problem** 1. You have been asked to use a new floor polisher but don't know how. Tell one thing you can do.

**Comment** _____

_____

_____

**Problem** 2. It is time to leave your work and you haven't cleaned up your area. Tell one thing you can do.

**Comment** _____

_____

_____